A LITTLE DECEPTION AMONG FRIENDS
"...THE SHORT STOURY (OUR STORY) CONVERSATIONS..."

**1 FEAR
GOD
LIFE** ™

One Fear, One God, One Life™ Publishing,
a division of S.A.I.N.T. International, Inc.
Alexandria, Virginia

A LITTLE DECEPTION AMONG FRIENDS

"...THE SHORT STOURY (OUR STORY) CONVERSATIONS..."

1 **FEAR**
GOD
LIFE ™

One Fear, One God, One Life™ Publishing
(a division of S.A.I.N.T. International, Inc.)
107 South West Street, Suite 285
Alexandria, Virginia 22314-2824
703.929.2164/2165
email: Van Saint @ aol.com; Lisa Saint @ aol.com

Book Cover and Chapter Concepts provided by
S.A.I.N.T. International, Inc.

10 9 8 7 6 5 4 3 2 1

ISBN: 0-9663279-0-X

For more information, correspondence, or to order additional copies,
please use the address and phone number above or fill out and mail an
order form in the back of the book...thank you.

FOREWORD

I invite you to envision your story's connection to these observations and impressions. I hope that you will appreciate that we share ourselves in many, many ways-. We are no stranger to one another than we are to ourselves and we are not nearly as strong apart as we are together. The blessings from the people who have shaped my life and living have also developed my belief and believing. We are bound to each other's successes and failures a bit more directly than we may have ever understood.

Maybe "deception" isn't such a bad thing, then, particularly among friends. We do it deliberately or not to adapt to situations we find comfortable or uncomfortable. Perhaps these actions are some sort of well-meant "dishonesty," to make a bad situation better or to make a good thing last. I think we act in these seemingly innocuous ways to protect ourselves until we truly know ourselves and that, if we could do this in a vacuum, no one would get hurt. Unfortunately, we try and fail and become frustrated with not doing better by our friends, our families, and ourselves. And so we deceive only the ones we think we care for the most. I hope that this exposition will help us to measure our deceptions with Atonement and relate, reason, and communicate with each other only in Truth.

This is a collection of stories, distilled into poetic verse, that tries to draw sensation and then sense to the front of your mind's eye. At the home of our soul and at the essence of our creation is the transcript of the conversation that God had and is having with each of us. What we are to become has already been placed within us--we only need to educate (or "draw from") that which we already have. My sincere hope is that as you read, you will enter into conversations and thoughts you have never had or have always had. And I hope that you will see and hear our truer connection and interdependence.

Thank you for "tuning in" and *listening*...

Derek

DEDICATION

Thank you to The Almighty God for enabling me to draw out of myself this one of the unlimited favors and blessings He has placed within me.

Thank you to My Queen, Lisa Sherrie, for our struggles and for our ultimate successes together--this work was incomplete before you!

Thank you to my Grandparents, Ollie and Evelyn Johnson, for providing the principles and strength for a family of families.

Thank you to My Uncle Michael Johnson and My Cousin Anthony Bell-- along with my Grandfather, you are my living heroes and examples of men.

And thank you to my Mother, Delores, for your heart and for my life.

...table of contents...

A LITTLE DECEPTION AMONG FRIENDS
"...*THE SHORT STOURY (OUR STORY) CONVERSATIONS*..."

...table of contents...(contd.)

I. IDENTIFICATION

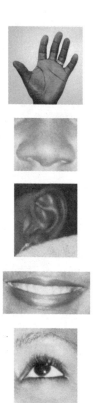

"...you have to be careful...

Deception (An Introduction, A Little Deception Among Friends, Part I)

We are the One we wish to become
for the unaware or unwary, the exit is also enticing,
the linger of scent or the residual of spent volleys,
the flash and fire of restriction or redemption

but the combination of lives and likes tantalizes the curious
and frustrates the ones who know
the collective incest of omission and isolation,
neglect and resolution
are now non-repeatable themes, spiked with features
frozen by the contrast of where they'd said they'd be,
but never did appear

instead, this beach, an accumulation,
an emulation of the best times we have ever had,
pitifully approximate our experience and recognition
and we must believe in this, as much as the wash of thought
over toes and the nape of the neck cleanses the dedicated
association we are prone to

Regarding our stigma, our warbling enigma
of trials and trails and trying to control the better way--
we want to stop lying to ourselves
to lessen the deception
we may well mean well, Consistent and minimally regretful
of what we do not understand
and yet continue to enjoy about each other

...of the effect you have on people..."

"...How do we prepare without the strength of a position?
Does the island submit to the ocean...

the Art of Life

If I scream softly will you still hear me through the nonsense
and will you be able to help me with what I am beckoning?
Though this may have very little to do with you,
I will need your assistance with the reckoning,
if not the destination

but if you were going with me, wouldn't we both know it?
just as I am to relinquish the journey,
the melodious trip and bump of invitation and rolling,
agreeable dis-chords propel us even further together,
though we are truly still apart

I am trying to expound upon the facts and not so much the analogies;
it is far more exciting and instructional
when I can distinguish the sensitive from the cynical
so when I do cringe, most of the time it is upon the broken, forced
slumber of my conscience, rocked by the tumult of yet another
indiscretion

I then wonder if I am a part of or apart from the village,
with baggage draped on either side of me;
I sit and balance myself and my motion
on a narrowly decrepit structure that will compel me or fell me one
day to a position that was preventable and not predestined

We are so much alike, the dissimilarities so glaring
so we love like fighters until there is no air left in the wind
leaving us helpless, breathless, lifeless to just think the way we like
to think things through and let our souls speak unchained so that
one day we, too, will understand that all we are doing is
misconstruing these gestures and symbols and flat illustrations
that are yet without any substance or depth

...submerging under the vast, relentless waves or does it withstand and resist and
refuse, to remain a refuge for the wayward...?"

"...we yearn to discern between the complement and the opposition,
but for the murky water and blood that separate now and then from us and them,...

Idle Time and Stray Thought

We, too, seek our own levels
and we are inclined to accept or adhere
because of our tolerance for mediocrity and safeguarding

we do not like words too much anymore, either
for we certainly haven't used them very much lately, rather
we listen to the continuum of rhythms and ranges and
communicate over time and this exercise exhibits our
example

it is the last song before the water falls,
a harpsichord of statements we make,
wet with moods created when we're all in love
when we all can talk about the same love

but we cannot belong only to ourselves
some elements of us are hopelessly imbalanced,
our war of wants and needs make us all minimally
something, depending on the phase of our thought

is the invisible intimidating?
Those whispers, sublime sentiments, and peripheral
problems that we can barely discern, feel and deal with;
do we understand or are we unnerved by their secrets, their
concealed connections to our conformity and
coordination?
will we be able to see our way out and above?

we rush with power and force together
as strong and certain as we read, run, and rehearse
our agendas, those dreams we seek to complete and do
but we cannot until we get true and figure out where to
search for what we have been missing

...it is the melding of our ambitions that sometimes pits us against ourselves..."

"...the significance is beyond and behind at the same time;...

The Prodigal Friend

the closer we are to the aftermath, the easier it is to step back and
away, but later, after our cooperation has fully subsided,
it becomes difficult to just sample the pain that is not ours--
even ours, if we just agree to ignore it otherwise

we are compelled to write the unseen
and to develop the obvious and the fleeting
these songs are inaudibly from the heart,
causing us to hear and doubt what we used to only confuse--
"hello," "goodbye," "come," and "go"--
and the fifth conversation only enables us to start reading again

it doesn't seem right to pray to God for the
evils we know we are going to do--shouldn't we just stop?
No, we protect and hoard and serve our little abeyances
until we feel the lash, the too sweet taste for what we should deny,
feeling we've *earned* this, all we could ever own, and it slips and we
slip behind, ashamed, until the next pass

but with all the access, how much air did *we* make today?
how limited, then, is our devotion but not the excess
we often resort to; Our plight is one of flight away from
our responsibilities and recklessness; the unquestionable answer to
our vaingloriousness will be too slow in coming as we continue to
lose on both sides of the equation and to make sure that nothing
bounds our emptiness, we appear to be waiting for something
that is in *front* of us
We may have to start from in between to begin to catch up,
forsaking some foundations and old structure, we deduce,
to properly acquaint and introduce
ourselves to the whole submissive story
and the discipline it will take to bring it to fulfillment

...so we steady ourselves with only our fingertips,
as we reach cautiously for the next ledge..."

"...there is a place must we prepare,
separate from our selfishness and apart from our animosity...

In Dependence (STOURy (OUR story), Part I)

we cannot remember the last time we let our hearts decide
but this time the promises are intended to be kept and this time
its light has flickered softly, warmly, urgently enough and has
kissed our minds; although the message was at first masked,
occluded by the distances between you and I, we have become
closer, connected to and by the heart of what matters to us both

you are to become my inside and I am to protect yours with the
armor of my soul; we will each first take care of ourselves, as we
have been all along, for we are no good to each other if we are not
first well; but if I happen to trip you, will you fall?
I will pick you up as often as you do--that's my end--
but yours is to learn not to stumble as often so that we may enter
into our progression, this the most important frustration

we are spiritual beings trying to live a physical existence, trying to
be *in* and not *of*, struggling to unclothe while we become
increasingly more comfortable with the cloak, more because it is
easier, more common and less disruptive; but the burden of this
duality will split and crush us, ashes to dust, if we are not careful

The incarnation of our incarceration, an incineration of our
otherwise ample aims, have become ashen shames of failure and
irresponsibility; Have we held those others so much, so closely and
guardedly that we can no longer walk, so that now and later, our
departure is shocking, triumphant, and tragic all at once and that,
after many years of striving, of starving, *suddenly* we have success..?

The memory softens all, the cuts become scrapes, the bruises
become brushes and the fire burns up as well as down--such a hard
way to grow up so fast and young--we did not know we were
bleeding (we thought it was just the rain) though there was too
much pain and attention that we were receiving and you provide
my cries, preside over my lies and lifeless courage until and into the
morning--We have to talk quickly for we have slept through the
comfort and cover of darkness and into the glare of our instincts
and friendly incest that finds us now corrupt, for like other things

that try to grow, too much essence is too much and we drown and
suffocate from the weight of water wasted--
we don't have time between washings to enjoy the slake--
we take *forgiven* as given until we are left dry

"...can I help or help heal you...?"--it was so clear and softly said
that we accepted without straining, forgiving, forgetting, and
recovering from the conditional or incomplete liaisons with every
other *plus* another that we have volunteered to suffer and so Love
and Mercy are among us and we are waiting for, but not wanting,
them to go -- so that we can "know" we were blessed, when we are
again without. So sometimes we wonder how much different we are
from what we have shown and we want to peek and peel back to
the intimacy and inhibition and whatever else lies unjostled,
unchallenged, just beneath, for whatever panting and ranting,
breathing and heaving we perform, the performances will lie there,
away but obstructing, indignant but instructing; we wonder how
much different we are when we are not

Independence has not come--can our individual "peaces" coexist?
The areas where we overlap and intercept we will have to negotiate
and consider our actions of peace that may conflict, stifle or bind,
for how can we draw on romance and vision with only one or two
hands? We need more time because we are wasting half of what we
have, having the effect of halving the effectiveness of our charge,
making us to foolishly consider loving each other and ourselves a
little less now so that we can be within that sanctuary a little
longer later, as if we can delay or postpone forever...

And so independence has not come, our absence has had an impact
on fondness and wonder; there are no strangers among us--our
stranger is within and that is which you already know about me
and I about you; we are each of each other's prayers, newborn
manifestations of our purest needs and we will die (again) without
provision, the duty that now stares us down, low, and hard. On
what will we defend? On what will we depend if we end up only
with our desires and without the mature silence and patience of
our dependence?; we can then control time and gravity-- if we can
only just wait and hold each other up

> *...to build our courage, to account for each other, our capacity,*
> *and our acceptability of ourselves..."*

*"...why is it that I never see your eyes until the morning, when they have been looking
at me all along? Is it because I did not want to see them...*

Remembering To Need To Believe and Deceive
(A Little Deception Among Friends in the STOURY (OUR STORY))
(The Inception)

we try to distance our conversations
from the tragedy and the betrayal
besetting our urges to kiss with
our urges to kill

our irresponsible play
with steel and matches still matches
and manages to still our manner;
We become angry and repulsed
with ourselves and by our own hands,
alarmed by our brutal responses as
the disenchanted and the disenfranchised

we are more easily spun, twisted and turned when we are flat
but to become erect, our foundation must be stronger,
heavier and deeper
to support the extreme, the supreme heights we are to attain,
to ward off the prevailing winds and the daily turbulence,
to stand against attacks, bumps and affronts--
and we may wobble but we will not fall

we are not brave--we just take those risks and chances and succeed
on our young faith,
which may make us seem foolishly lucky or lucky to be so foolish,
childlike and thus protected from Within
but we think that we know
at least as much
as the fools among us...

...for what they would tell me about myself?.."

II. ACKNOWLEDGMENT

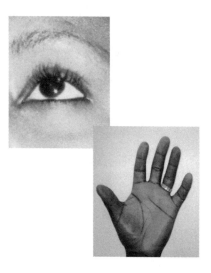

"...The Top Ten Terms Of Deception...

A Little Deception Among Friends (Part II)

what's a little deception among friends
given the protection and definition
you find in their company

the defense of games and dreams is
as transient as thoughts in spring
the priorities shift and stop, seemingly
as extensions of time and patience and interest,
signaling the deflection of love into acceptance
and the defection of denial to rejection

through this discovery and search,
we find sense and levity, counsel and adoration
of what we suspect and detect in each other

in the differences there are consolations
and everyone receives something they did not expect
the contrasts and excitement beckon the exotic
as we construct and tear down,
appreciate and overlook
monuments to our impossibly mutual satisfaction--
we cannot win, lose, or commit
if we do not first share a little deception

        ...*10.* ...*never...*
          9. ...*Always...*
          8. ...*I can't...*
          7. ...*I'm afraid...*
          6. ...*I promise...*
          5. ...*I love you...*
          4. ...*I hate you....*
          3. ...*in all honesty...*
          2. ...*tomorrow...*
          1. ...*it's impossible..."*

"...can we understand and interpret silence...

Fearless

does fear make us evolve, resolve, or involve others in our misery
and do we perpetrate our conditions and the static with some
status
and are we at least "pretendingly" friendly
while we eat and serve a little bit of poison
(with some acid to wash it all down)
So that maybe we are not afraid at all

or do we devolve to our desperation instead of our aspiration
and increase the limits we start with already
So maybe we are not afraid at all

we implicate and assimilate loyalty with guilt
some portion of this and then half more again
our receipt and transmission is wry and subliminal,
we cry "criminal" against those who do what we allow
the vulnerable intimidators among us, venerable stimulators
who christened this temple of thieves
So we toil and toy with the possibilities--do we spare or do we
spoil?
At least we have given thought
So maybe we are not afraid at all

The scary areas of our lives are melodious and methodical
for their nature and threads are woven into our faces and heads
we cannot recognize the broke, bent, and beveled, stained and
leveled
aspect of our common-ness--this does not even cause us to stare
the opulence of the offenses and assaults arrest us not
So maybe we are not afraid at all

we do covet and kill and lie
Even those of us who are front and righteous,
if perhaps not centered
we accept speed over accuracy too easily and upset ourselves,
blindingly astonished, when the spatial references impact like a
suddenly immediate vacuum and we walk on (by), now with
inhibition, prohibition, catharsis and dogma
So maybe we are not afraid after all

In spite of our faults, is there something we can boast?
Can we host or entertain respect for the attempted failure at
the uniform which has never embraced us before
we have utilized silence as science and graduated well,
well below the uneven standards we have set,
wistfully, before ourselves
though few and far between, we have had our chances
with so many recalls since the last ultimatum
and too many requests before the next--
So maybe we are not afraid anymore

Did we sense some sincerity? Maybe a sweetly light, persistent and
terminal resistance to nonsense?
Our passion, our patience allows us to tell more of, more than,
the rest of the story because we are unsure of our next time,
we take pittances for our sanity
and it is not enough to balance our deficiencies
that impart or enable aggression
against those who do not know any better
So we proceed (recede) to each other's graves not knowing
that maybe no one's afraid--maybe that's the case--
and maybe our fear is what we most waste...
Anymore

... or do we need whispers and suggestions
to move our opinion, which, without action, is ignorance...?"

"...one mirror's distance separates us,
but we are careful not to sit and sense for too long...

This Is Faith

the little part of us that dies everyday
is evil anyway
for the first time again
we understand how innocent
we once were
there is too much trouble affecting our thoughts
and we must pray
for energy away from the source--
We must not stay too long
for it will not remain forever

the presence of our few weakened spirits,
here and not in our true home,
we do not savor this too long,
but we save ourselves
for where we need to be

The resistance rubs up against us and our sides
We are comfortably familiar with the danger,
more grace than mischief in our aims
We revere the natural gifts
and utilize them as intended,
for giving and for forgiving

when we next meet, let us gather ourselves quickly,
to close the degrees of our commitment--
because we truly believe and know
we will stand up and witness
beyond the walls and doors
of the secure and acceptable
this is our only way
this is all we have--
for this is faith

...for the way we see the way we look would make us hesitant to move again..."

"...the appearance of the threat should not make us vigilant..

KILLJOY WAS HERE

let us bathe in our sentiment
not the sediment of what we have discovered in ourselves
and not in what made us happy for the moments beyond the
comfortable, uncommon silence we share now

The resistance of a free spirit, the tannin of our interaction and
mischief, is a mildly brutal and harsh paradox of our previous
manipulations, doing what we should not and knowing what we
do,
We are frustrated and empty, not in sequence, but in total
as we find pleasure in pleasure *and* pain, left only with
a subjective example of our dependence and contempt

This is a retaliatory story, we suppose, an opposing memory of the
news that was fiction after all
we have been ruined in so many good ways
so we take precautions that increase and attenuate
turning our docile, aspirated respite into nonchalance
as we pick up our shields and swords

But it is not an invasion if we have invitation
no matter how we respond to what we are supposed to do
we are not sure if we want that kind of clarity at this point
this absence prevents the indignation of my tender deficiencies,
austere like this brazen day
we are exasperated and cavalier, satisfied and tempted by our
selfish pursuits and reckless avoidance
and we are so sorry
that we were so happy
about that then

...by then, it is too late..."

"...the rue of the fall and the frozen keeps the aching senses alert, revived...

Pride/Precision (INTIMACITY, Part I)

I love the way you think
how you are sensitive when I am not
the manner in which you love me
through my contradictions and reasons

when I think of you
there is a reaction and promise
I just want you in my thoughts
to understand that we are
Still

I just wanted to hear
that you would be careful
unintentional, with my heart .
the selfishness runs
between what is mine and yours and back again
and I don't want to lose it again
in the confusion

while I wait at the summit
I close my eyes and stand in the peacefulness
as you close behind me and surprise me just a bit
I peek down, for our hands are one for awhile
and I smile easily now
because it was lonely trying to get to heaven
without you

...there have only ever been two distinctions--
those that lose and the survived..."

"...but even the attempts have been feeble, severely lacking in impact,
value and significance,...

IsReal

they abridged and erased behind themselves the thick line between
love and hate, traversing and cursing the disbelieving state of us,
the brutally affected, whose hallowed, hollowed-out bodies and
souls meet and do not cross the brevity of our sojourn

every day has been a new record, a mark repeatedly eclipsed by our
foregone ability to stand and breathe freshly, if not truly.
This is rare only insofar as it was always unexpected,
for we were not lost until they *told* us we were and forced us to *be*
and we did not accept those lies until we believed them
and not until we began to "teach" ourselves in the same way

where is this place and to whom does it truly belong?
we debate over the *chosen*
when the questions really concern the *worthy*
how nearly we have come and become the antithesis to the
proclamation, our self-inoculation of a faith and illusion
we were meant to master

we were trained forward to nullify the shock effect of our exodus
but we reasoned after the fact, concluding that we could have
waited for help to come, to have swum instead of waded,
tied to a preservation based on reliance--but if we could have
afforded to wait, wouldn't we also have had the time to help
ourselves?
These veins are not the same, but they are attached to the same
source and aim

like babies in new, shallow water, we crawl softly and smoothly
away from the dilapidated shells of ourselves, rehabilitated,
rejuvenated as the turmoil and erosion slackens as our exteriors
become more like stones, not hardened, but protective,
solid from the inside out--where, upon which,
and how our future might be built

...the sincerity and intimation provide neither substance nor foundation
for the later trials and tests--but if we never get there, was it worth the pain...?"

"...we give all to a point where comfort is threatened...

ATALANTA (STOURY (OUR STORY), Part II)

this is our story
of worry and horror that we do not soon yield or forget
for what should have never been taken cannot ever be given back--
it must also be seized and raped of the glory and purity
we have never enjoyed here

many, many years have provided this mixture,
this message that encourages and repudiates,
persuades and pursues, deifies and defies
we have grown up and been taught in the middle of the worst for
so long that it was natural to scratch out an existence
and to be happy with that-- until we learned of revolution--
what proof can we give of our faith, conviction,
and courage if we do not first free ourselves?
the question is of being affirmed from the evil perspective,
no matter how sensuous, versus what we knew
and how we do from within

we are of one mind though we appear disjointed
and in direct contention with one another,
standing outside of our and spirits whispering vituperatively of
communion and bloodshed; we cleave honestly yet cautiously
for this is the only bond we have any more
and it is diminishing rapidly

many will come a little later but they will last a little longer
we will only need to break the unwilling--
we will have to teach the willing a little better
because when the remaining choice is escape
what hope do we have of agreement
our ambitions and conditions have crept into recession
and our possession, when compared to our challenge
is now at the very bottom.

...and we back away to the quiet refuge of our knowing glances
and nodding, unspoken approvals..."

III. CONFESSION

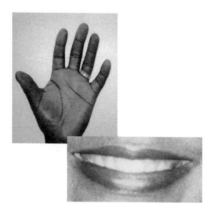

—

.

"...We do not keep each other's secrets very well or for very long,...

Desperation (A Little Deception Among Friends, Part III)

what is it that you fear most, the truth in humor
or the humility of finding some truth
in the lie...?

Our right eye senses deception right away,
though the picture is compliant, compassionate,
its composition is sufficiently compartmented by
another, different vision

and what of the pain from honesty
or of feelings salvaged by a kinder, gentler distortion--
is this any more or less wrong?

We still build on love and insight
while eroding the structure with confusion,
distress, and distrust
so that even the concern depreciates,
but it never stops.

The stark contrasts
among what we want, what we think, and what we need
are beyond ourselves, our self-interest,
and our selective actions

we offer not liability and distance and divorce
but an examination,
and whether we stand together, in unison or opposition
we remain
on the same side...on the same side
of desperation

*...taking turns with our false references that untruss and force us
between the choice of our dreams and what must do everyday..."*

"...when I knew you for days, we had talked for years, soul to soul, heart and mind
linked by an original, pure, and complete proposition...

Passion

...not compassion or compression
it is actual and action within, protected, the way you consider my
thoughts--this is what I will say, this is exactly my essence,
overriding myself and my immaturity

Passion, not sensation or cessation,
at the core of everything that I do and what I do not--I will thank
you not eventually, but now for this revelation and invite you to
the realization; I have no memory except of ideas which have been
wrong, all along, in meaning and purpose
and in the vision that I might shape for others to see

Passion, not suppression or succession
of touch, love, and worry beyond worthiness, but short of complete
happiness--when I learn to like myself more, I will like you better
and when I learn to love myself completely, I will be able to share
myself and in love with you--what I am lacking is what I am
missing is what I have is what I need from me, from you

Passion, expression not confession
and simply more than paper and ink; it is the deep, the essential
bridge of blackness between isolation and desire, with exits to
perception where the truth changes, while what we think and
believe and judge does not. the difference between sensible and
surreal is that which satisfies, and this is what we keep

Passion and Intensity, the way I need love from you, to learn and
to grow; it is the source of my other, unrequited fear; my trust in
you to build and not except the urgency that is electric to me
currently, exciting my awareness of intimacy

Passion, the taste in the air the aroma close behind my eyes
and around my ears I inhale deeply again for a breath, for the
words*patience, forever* and *permission*
to share as much Passion as we want

...that led us out of our deception and darkness..."

"...we are crowded in between values that do not belong to us...

No (The Politeness of No)

I'm not sure which was sweeter
your lips or your voice, the wish or the choice of satisfaction,
gratification, or submission
you have moved me, swayed with me and pushed me gently,
starting, going, interrupting my hesitation with encouragement and
presence--always your presence

I like to remember our exchanges,
our free transfer of the powerful and potent multiple meanings
and desires we moderate with our respect for a genuine pursuit of
welfare and altruism
and we are also aware of our past betrayals

we dreamt all of a sudden about those sentiments that we liked
best and remembered most
we smiled to shield ourselves,
protecting our time and countenance,
reassuring ourselves against the darkness

and then the night screamed up at us to continue, the breezes
billowing our resolve ever so slightly as trees bent and limbs
moved, pressed forward into life we should be, stepping between
ideas and pools of mischief
and we watched and wondered when we would speak to, stop and
console each other, hopefully,
before we were too far along

...so how can we accept the apologies of what has never been put forward...?"

"...until the last return, we cannot rest; until the last have heard,..."

Intention

We are just pretending
because none of this has ever really happened,
yet we have to persuade ourselves,
delude ourselves into thinking that this madness
and pretension is real

whose voice do we hear when no one is speaking
what is the inflection and how is the clarity--
does it mumble or stumble
or tumble down over what we were thinking?
And have we ever been truly in love
or have we just loved and been loved
we suspect that we pass through this fantasy
for short respites and retreats
from what we have to live and like
until we awaken or retire and shelter ourselves
from responsibilities imposed upon us
by our own volition and omission

without handles or steady hands
we attempt to control each other
with our prominence and protocol
instead of our intervention and care
but in the course of protection,
we wait and play and delay and stay
the onset of what we identify as identity
but are afraid to accept and challenge.

...we must continue to press forward with the work..."

"...after all we have done together, it is now that we are committed to being friends;
we no longer love as eagerly, we no longer seek redemption so quickly,...

Only The Mistakes Are Mine

So where do I stand, in a pulpit or in prayer
and the truths that come to me, including my own--
which ones will finally guide my final direction?

there is now more focus and patience than I have known for some
time, sometimes speaking to me from a language I had forgotten
it speaks to my heritage, my true nature and makes me tremble
with embarrassment and confusion,
given the history I would have considered immutable

Who I am at this moment and the next certainly is constant
energy, changing its example,
but the continuum does define my freedom
to maneuver through the next sequence
sudden movements to ambivalence is not the purpose for breathing
this life, this breath,
this gift of responsibility that has timing, urgency, and respect,
save for the fool I used to be and who would have been among the
dead and the transient

but if I fail to steer my reference out of fear, sincere reverence or
revolt, I am still willing to learn and submit
I just do not understand how much and for whom yet
I'm not sure of the way, the path forsaken for the trail I am to leave

But to the assured success, I'll gladly adhere and acknowledge
and one day I will prove myself worthy to myself--
but until then--
only the mistakes are mine

...we no longer hurt as maliciously, and we need not touch each other
in that way again--and in this way we succeed..."

"...our definition is not as distinct as the shared sorrow between us...

Concession

Where risk exists
there is position to establish
but it is across
the unstructured into the defined;
we are against that which we want
and we are together for that which is already ours
whether this is special or a coincidence
and whether it has a purpose and an agenda
we give and take and receive and keep

the voice of reason
is less than the voice of vision or the sense of
passion and we breathe in the melody and script
and balance and harmony that draws patience into
tolerance and consideration from commitment
the comfort seems too much and almost uneasy
because where I want to be is with you,
far from complacency,
very close to content, the content
of our intentions...

...and neither is the memory between us that we have yet to make,
sustain, and live for..."

"...we exclusively avoid those joyous and persuasive gatherings, the truths of our
failures to reach goals and protection...

The Crab Theory
(STOURY (OUR STORY), Part III)

light drops into this slick cylinder from time to time
an indignation to us because we cannot enjoy its warmth,
too busy with our loud talking and scratching and
Stubborn and relentless, we do not even have the lack of
absence we do not even have this-- we do not even exist

how many battles must we survive before we can rest,
push and coast away from the pain that has kept us honest
it is the internal strife we suffer from the most
struggling and competing against each other, faking or
pretending until we are on our way to wherever we can go
Do we smile, shiver, or shudder as we look around and
wonder and see ourselves for ourselves,
but not in any mirror

there are thin lines between imagination and conscience
Assumption and fact separate the Disinterested,
with their self-inflicted scales and scars, from the Provident
and the Prudent, with their cause and repudiation, from
the Unorthodox and Aggressive, who lack understanding
and cooperation--and All are prone to consumption

we have no stability, no station, though the surroundings
are constant; the wake of our neighbors jolts us and we in
turn disrupt the brave and the sweet who merely want a
chance at the rope swinging deliciously or deleteriously as a
lifeline or a lynch, for it does not matter--they, we, only
long for refuge and escape, whatever the cost
Our bodies cry out for air and liberation--we just want to
be able to be and to reach and to reach back more often, if
we could still have hands to feed with, to succeed with
after we have ascended

...and submission to a consistent standard--
so we just disappoint now, rather than kill..."

IV. REPENTANCE

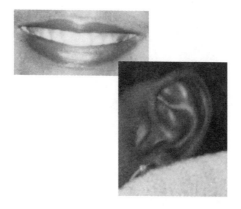

"...we have loved ideally and without one heart; more ethereal than satisfying,...

The Deep Abyss of Shallowness
(A Little Deception Among Friends, Part IV)

a shallow protocol uncovers
the impossible symphony of denouement and denial
and we get there and away to a sense of perfection and friendship,
beyond fears imagined and proposed,
translated into chords and choruses
we'd rather not admit

striking, scratching, shooting though the surface
the ritual is an habitual loop of life we
stop, step into and out of at will
controlling, too, the invaluable freedom of inactivity
an authority executed without discretion, justification, or need
we continue to dream of enacting our desires,
delving a bit deeper in our confrontation,
through this thin film of restraint
that keeps us from ourselves,
each other, and our invincible strength

and suddenly we are dying
it is the sleep we covet
a soulful slumber dieting our
worthiness and success,
with the superficial and the super-physical frames of ego and lust
where more is only and just more
but far less, and maybe just
what we need

*...our wishes wafting so eloquently and sensibly, easing pain into the
subconsciousness, to the point of acceptance and yearning..."*

"...each time that haze stops on the horizon,
like a still soiled blanket hung out to dry,...

Bruise Therapy (Instinct, Part I)

what if everything we could ever do we could never do again--
and what of those things we never did get to--
would we wink or shrug and promise or
just say no because we had been hurt too much?

We cover down, abreast of our questions
walking strongly and feigning the way we truly feel
but if we could feel better about ourselves
it would show the uneven pressure of the vice,
the immoral vise, the device of this life
the sweat and blood that pounds inside and around you
swells into bewilderment, dismay and destruction
but is it the creature or creation that we will allow to devour us?

we ask permission for safe passage
and do not consider our own power to heal from within
our too lonely soles whimpering, our two lonely souls wallowing,
wishing we had help when we walk alone
with our spirits slogging through,
sloughing off the encumbrances and encounters
that do not serve us well enough

During this resting piece, we are resisting peace
as we sit out on the plain and scream
protecting our heads from the divots and abrasions,
those unusual occasions
that heal our minds for the next time,
the next time we feel, or feel we have to fight...

...there is a glare that somehow forces itself through
and my eyes sting just a little bit for a long time..."

"... 'DEAD'--definition--...

DREaD SCOTT

it is time to move on, but once you have been misdirected,
can you even know where to begin again
when the beginning was all wrong...?

Has there ever been a reversal, not of the statement nailed forever
to the hands of our ability and confidence, but of the resignation
and deprivation of minds pitifully wrapped in and warped by a
self-proclaimed supremacy?

Perhaps there was an attempt, feeble and official
to massage the tender adult and assuage the kings to assent,
temporarily, to the sublime and conceptual overrule
of the over-referenced and the granted, because if we have to rely
on this law and its retractions to help us
We are Failed

These withdrawals dissipate and still end with our holocaust,
designated as an unfortunate mishap of history
And this is how a people could be depraved, how a people could be
deprived and still comport and deport themselves without each
other in gain and loss and wealth and poverty

We are entitled to our natural environment and habitat,
away from the animals they think *we* are
where we can be at home and own our serenity
though we are able to move and run (because we have had to)
we may wish to step back, out and aside to watch as phases and
faces pass and remain oblivious to the lurches and leers past us,
impenetrable at last because we know ourselves
and not the identity, classification, or place
that they want us to accept

...not performing that function for which it was created..."

"...if we could eat whenever, whatever, however we wanted,
when could we ever be hungry enough...

Weak from Yesterday

the way we go and could have gone, the songs we sing or should
have sung; many days we are so sick and tired and stupid for
suffering like this, for pushing and pulling, scratching and digging,
all for a time that has already passed

...youth when we are old and pleasure when there is pain
knowledge when we are confused and peace when we are at war
silence when there is chaos and solace when there is despair
strength from the work against the weakness of yesterday

These are just more old words nevermore spoken, read or said
like today's sun that burned out and away but when we see it
tomorrow our eyes will ache with eyelids that flutter and snap in
disbelief or disapproval, the same ones that bat and dance during
the failure of our free pursuit-- we are the ones that pranced, then
sat, and then tired all too soon...

...youth when we are old and pleasure when there is pain
knowledge when we are ignorant and peace when we are at war
silence when there is chaos and solace when there is despair
strength for the work against the weakness from yesterday

our provision should be happier, for each one and each other
but begging and guessing and disagreeing and disappointing
have not kept us so calm, so far; it is endurance that we need,
to drive faster without learning to drive, to build without first the
building of the bricks and we can wait for a mission that we can
return to, that can, in turn, return us...

...youth when we are old and pleasure when there is pain
knowledge when we are ignorant and peace when we are at war
silence when there is chaos and solace when there is despair
strength from the work against the weakness for yesterday

...to dig and scratch at a hint or a clue or a buried piece of coin or precious metal..."

"...we can hear the echoes of our own voices from the time before...

Instinct

How would you feel if your hands were gone?
What about the ordinary acts, the missing,
the emptiness where once there were gifts and construction

Where would you stand if you no longer had feet?
Not the station, location, or what,
but how since you could linger no longer like before;
what if you were truly rooted, relegated to stumping "steps"
where once you gracefully or guardedly trod

What would you see if you had no eyes,
darkness and deprivation were your only light,
except that for which you trained your other senses to compensate

What would you do with the space voided by your heart
after you no longer had use for it?
The hollow echo that used to whine and pout, gently beckoning,
begging, anxious for anticipation and satisfaction

Could you recover from all of these mistakes?
Starting anew, sowing the pieces and fragments that composed you
into you again; could you fully apply yourself as second hand,
the second chance but without
the enforced errors of your former ways...

Or would you simply slump, like a flickering lump of a candle,
unable to handle, ramble or burn for much any more..?

*...and we can remember the movements and places
we have now replaced and moved away from..."*

Theomachy (it's just noise)

If you can't do and you can't teach
then you're just making noise
even with direction and focus,
you exist on a periphery that
keeps getting bigger and more consuming
to the unassuming
who pretend to make a difference
but it's really just noise
not even talk where there is
at least minimal reliance
on promises probably not kept or intended
and not action because action is tangible,
descriptive and oriented to means and ends,
however counter or acceptable to the judgment
and not progressive either--
a miring of time and resources against
the leaden notion of eternal, perpetual preparation
to sing or to teach, preach or do for self
to draw, write, or copy
the objective is to create, regular and useful
to you and how, not what--
otherwise it's just noise
pushed further and further away
from us and our peaceful serenity
and blissful awareness

"...and I may have to finally wait for what will comfort me wholly...

Slumber Party (STOURY (OUR STORY), Part IV)

this is a somber story of how we die as we live
and as victimlessly as possible yet the carcasses remain,
walking examples and statuettes of the desecration

at first glance, the distance seems to close with our every advance,
but we are slipping into jeopardy towards a blindness
we will never see coming

the torture and confinement is perverse because we abet and aid
those who were *first* irresponsible and we want them to *want to* fix
the situation according to our inadequate comprehension of the
way we should be

music and words and dereliction and death
perform during this minstrelsy and we watch, not unlike a
reflection, but a type of impression that keeps us back and
crawling, though we are capable of standing up and forward--
there is a gathering going on, but perhaps we should pass

and though we should sleep and nap, we cannot afford to,
so tiresome are the opinions of how and who and we dance on
tables, entranced by the shapes of lamps and lanterns that *can*
perform other functions, for more people, for more purpose

to look at the celebration, we could continue to survive
and sing along or realize that we have heard all of these songs
before and felt the gyrations that knot our strides and insides and
that somehow, before twilight and after dawn
we are pale and drawn and gone
and it is so very very early
to be so very very dark

...and not just through the night..."

V. ATONEMENT

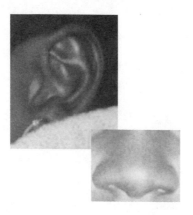

"...we have written several pretty songs,
but we hope that the angels and saints among us can hear what we have written...

The Late Song (A Little Deception Among Friends, Part V)

the world only twirls halfway around
before it starts back the other way
And try as we might,
we cannot fight the forces that make us look forward
to this familiar failing the next time

We bounce inside and we are bound by this incubation,
an isolation that keeps you from you and me from me and us
We have lingered too long and have long been forgotten,
like the rest of the cluttering items--we lessen ourselves more,
hopelessly, in this battle between the free and the willing

Sometimes, though, we listen quite neatly, read and read into each
other none too discretely, each bleeding into our own ambition,
trust, and hesitation
It gets late earlier now, though there is more light that gives
direction, although it does not dictate the way
so we stay busy looking at what we should be doing, wondering,
wandering about during sleep, wondrous sleep

We are somewhere between the secular and the secure,
torn by an opposition of our dreams and visions
we have exposed in prose and posed to those who cannot possibly
fathom the solution to the equation--
our power is and will forever be mental,
elemental thought and speech,
balanced by acts and deeds random and kind

...and dare not say or think, really,
for ruin would follow and we would surely despair..."

"..we have suffered to be apologetic..

Pray (for the Queen)

we have longed to be, eternally, long before we ever knew of each
other or at least for as long as we care to remember
we can perform all manners of sensation and cessation,
and still be without this placidness
we poke and peer at for moments at a time

I hear what you think, I write what you imply
I fear what you do not and I need what you are
I need who you are to become complete and to complement you

we have fought for submission
Doing what we'd both rather not envy or espy, experiencing the
spectacle more than once

I hear what you think, I write what you imply
I fear what you do not and I need what you are
I need who you are to become complete and to complement you

how do we learn or do we just accede and apply
to some position or partial possession of peace, completed by our
conditions and confessions...?

I hear what you think, I write what you imply
I fear what you do not and I need what you are
I need who you are to become complete and to complement you

we have been each other's shepherd, listening and doing, hearing
and responding, reporting and exemplifying the best impressions
and the most daunting appearances and contrivances
we have tended each other more properly, more privately and
purposefully than we could have ever imagined

I hear what you think, I write what you imply
I fear what you do not and I need what you are
I need who you are to become complete and to complement you

we have been high and low across the waste, the wasted land and
sway of lazy, idling imaginations and actions better left aside;
inside I feel more satisfied than I have been, with you, with myself,
without the presence of the tryst that was "you" and "I" and "the
others" that we ran from and toward
We have changed, maybe exchanged our minds,
not from or for one instance to another but in theory of and
practice about the ways of moments,
those exceptions of life we have been involved in

I hear what you think, I write what you imply
I fear what you do not and I need what you are
I need who you are to become complete and to complement you

we have turned hard to the right,
each of us hardly right without the other, our offerings of loyalty
and guilt have given way to a love
that is finally on the same side of our curiosity

so let's talk about less talk
politely, sweetly and lightly, like we have said before
letting those parts of you fit neatly into me and me, wholly, into
you
as we reveal and reconcile our versions of fulfillment and truth,
from this new house,
from here,
our prayer

I hear what you think, I write what you imply
I fear what you do not and I need what you are
I need who you are to become complete and to complement you

...for our reparations behind the broken door to our stolen dreams..."

"...it is better to fall out in love...

Does Sound Rise or Fall?

It falls like naked petals upon the soft body of doubt
and rises with the short, hastened breaths of trust from moments of
short satisfaction and only moments of encouragement
and if it falls upon the unwanted or the unwilling,
did it ever rise at all?
the ascent lost upon the resting place,
dying unembraced, unenchanted, and uncalled
this is what love sounds like
and how it feels to believe
and know
and receive
But to understand, extend your hands
to the resurrection
of life from within

...than to fall out of love or to fall from love completely...?"

"...Our plagues are but questions for which we have not the proper prayer;
our salvation, so precious...

Rain (Part One, *The Opening Shower*)

the rush began as a trickle,
short trips and drops of movement that came and succumbed
to their isolation and consolation

our Understanding came secure and stout in two stages of
development, though there can only ever be *one first* house--
it is here that we listen to each other--
the other exists when we yell that we are both wrong and we never
do discuss the truth, but then maybe it depends on which part we
most fully understand

we missed each other more after the second time we lost ourselves
in loss-- but what about the last time?
Did we feel it or did we conceal it,
hiding the event from anyone attending,
relieving the waste of whispers and teases and tastes through
speech, scripture, and position?
We may not touch the perfect texture of
loft and love and less more than once
in a thousand times
but if we can reveal our lives in the glory of the rain
we may at least cleanse the wounds of our shame

...is ebbing where it should flow, only oozing where it should run like rapids..."

"...a delicate signal that pierces the night; the western sunrise that rises unnoticed;
the voice from home that is remembered and not heard;
the imagination and conscience of the world...

L-LAMENTS

I miss you from
somewhere deep inside my body,
closer to the very center of my soul
every picture is you
each new place is somewhere
we have been together
the fragrance of the next moment
the smell of the next season
it is you
all
over again

a slow awkward dance it has been
with you only in my mind--
outside of my reach
I cannot miss you anymore
for there is no more to give from here
wrap your thoughts around
me now as I sleep
and take care of my heart, my love, my love
until we dream once together again

...the summer innocent with new experience; the sense and despair of persistent
separation; the graceful beckoning of spirit and soul;
and the simple complicity of love..."

"...desire me in your thoughts and your conceptions, but not simply as a love...

Girl Friend (2 in a Million, Part 1)

we fight like lovers
but the punishments and embraces we lace ourselves with
bind us and our interpretation of what we are
and what we are not

things have been difficult with me today
and it is your fault
only because you are so close and culpable and you know so much
about the roots of my escapades and tirades,
how I once made a point to make a point

will we see each other differently each time we meet or will we
excavate and reveal the mishaps of our concert, misshapen and
mistaken, perhaps, for our generally bitter origins and, at once,
our interaction is sanctified-- otherwise, it is sabbatical
we stall into each other comfortably
talking, singing, crying, and slowing down to assess
because we never (will) have enough time (together)
We act out of doubt, we ache with the debt of knowing and
our best creations are metaphorical dreams and relations
as obtuse as tree-strobed light, some irregular diffusion
of inspiration and instinctiveness that governs or maybe arrests our
attempts to step and not jump when we *know* we could bounce, if
we happen to be too far away from safety and security

what we give each other freely is as emotionally perfect as we will
ever be, the illumination of dark sides that are really only shadows
Our reasons for breathing, even dreaming alone, no longer exist;
these dependencies, exchanges, and connections are as foreign and
fleeting as the romance and riches we used to seek
But now the description of our default impugns the definitions of
our faults--we are ecstatic and excited just to share isolation and
bittersweetness just in case we turn around,
sooner than we expected, into the very end

...because you and your mind have made me much more than that..."

"...we share and shear the accuracy of our indulgences...

New Share's Day (STOURY, (OUR STORY), Part V)

and so this is trust
what I have believed in
searched for, accepted and lost
in the window transparent, reflective,
broken and cracked
exclusive, inviting, tempting, and forbidding
I react and follow
not selfish but sensitive symbols
showing not saying
with heart and eyes, souls and ears open
to be careful, receptive, respective and wary
to carry the share of respect and revelation
toward our day committed, yes committed now
to growing and maturing

the understanding of differences
whether leading or led
it is not what is said
There are feelings we cannot touch
And there is a warmth we cannot feel
visions we cannot see
one we may never truly be
for the possibilities are better
by two
by two who
exchange completely
our position, advantage, submission
what we have given
is given back
and we are better now
than how
we found each other

...and we rest uncomfortably in our resulting indifference..."

VI. FORGIVENESS

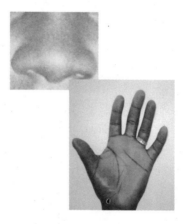

"...from the beginning there was one tomorrow--now that the end has come to pass,
the bluster of those speaking wildly steadily increases your vulnerability...

To Remember (A Little Deception Among Friends, Part VI)

we were concerned
so we decided to develop ourselves first,
separate and disposed among the enemy
we chose correctness and construction
from within our own borders
that we must tear down from the inside out
and truly explore the newness we have owned forever
that we, now together, have not...

we shall prepare and live this awareness
without friction
our memory of old methods and manners
shall be short and proper
and we will be joyful as we expect and earn our full
honor, original destiny, and peace

we may no longer suffer the crimes of
the forsaken before we have been justly accused or
ignored for ignorance is the presence of absence
we tell each other this so that we will know it
for an eternity
for the time we will have to remember

...wishes and dreams and hopes and things were never much worth keeping protected.
The thoughts were always uncovered, discovered, long before any intent was clear..."

"...we might have changed something or some things...

These Last Days With You

why did you stay
when I gave you reasons to go
how should I have known or seen
what you had created and kept?

I can still touch your heart from here
and I can hear my own beating
if I stop what I am doing or thinking
and remain in you

my fingers pulse with the flow of lost touch and control,
this fear and anxiety raging like laughter
and I begin to realize the warm flight of you through my thoughts

we can move closer to make sense of the noise--
we have more time now
you are so much to me and everyone you touch closely,
with happiness and compassion

what did you see then and now
your eyes openly secreting away what you desire and shame,
your tears falling sweetly like ounces,
anointing my ignorance

the measure of love
is such ado about something
and our lives could pass in great sections at a time and I could regret
never showing you that I know that I care; but we will take care of
ourselves --by ourselves--
until we can together again

...after we had talked and cried and we thought and spoke some more..."

"...and though this may be unfair to say, I say it anyway...

Loveletters to a Friend

And my heart dropped
because I thought you were being arrogant and indifferent,
about its care and protection
but, yes, I have heard of your intentions, the suspension had
let me down too easily for you must understand
what it takes for me, what it took from me,
to give up, to give in and wait for the wish to pass through
the uncertain stances and dances
and finally into our cradle

So secretly may we now begin,
guilt and risk dripping off our lips and shoulders like so many
burdens released; but now that we speak it,
what do we do with our responsibility?

This is where I will hesitate because we have been careful or
fortunate not to offend or offer too much, but just enough,
for the pity we may need to feel later

There is just a twinge of pain, a slight strain,
perhaps because I have not yet arranged my wants and needs
with yours and the limits of what you will give to me,
share with me
I understand the yearning to be nearer, but how much closer,
in how many ways, can we be?
You see, this is where you must be clearer
so that I may understand these conditions
and if they still exist
we will never be all that we want
until we yield all that we thought we had
and breathe for and feed the love we've borne

...and pray you'll forgive me and this personal trespass..."

"...tonight was the best we would ever be...

AMIAN
(This Is Faith, Part II)

Show me water
the kind that purifies
and makes me whole
the resource that clears
and gives
that runs quickly through
the tenuous clasp of unsure hands
water that escapes during the
waltz of worry and anticipation
the kind that shimmers
brighter than never before
during the course of new rains in new
summers and that, after calm collection
we can rejoice in sharing
not just in receiving
the tide that washes
us up together, much closer than before
show it to me that I may,
of want and accession, drink humbly
because Faith needs help, too...

...until it passed into our memories and the 'next best' that we now desire..."

"...palms and praises have placed us...

Flowers (...sending flowers)

...to your spirit and its soul, you grow and flourish
from soil saturated by achievements and upsets but bright,
like you, this is yours, a harvested bounty of courage and
concern, breathing in and purifying the evil that plagues us,
generating clearer air for the floundering, the forlorn...

If we cannot be quiet, can we have consistent and regular
noise, for there is some peace in that,
where we can appreciate each other for this space,
but hate each other's use of it
It is so much easier to be honest when we don't seem to care

we can prance around
on broken needles and glass with cold, frozen feet
striving twice as hard to be equal with the very least
instead of kicking up the very dust within ourselves,
that *is* ourselves,
the essence of the dance and music of our creation

Would we place our palms over what and how we hear,
here, where we have impaled ourselves,
flailing ourselves about the lies we can live with
and lives we can do without

our arms are open wide
and we are coated with the fine pollen-sugar of our breaths
we still could not move closer toward, forward, or over
and pooling all around us was only hope
the hope that if our sending flowers anything,
let our anything be true...

...beyond the images and into the substance..."

"...because I know now not to worry about incidents and accidents...

NISA (Girlfriend, Part II)

I wish I had written to you earlier, sooner
but I wouldn't have been ready enough, would you?

So now we are us and this is thus,
sad roses followed by the wait that was not so lonely--
so maybe it was you--now that you are here
and then you were not

I'd often wish you were patient enough
to hear my impatient stories and storied
patter so you could know that it should be you
now that I am ready (are you?),
And is this the matter?

Your speech is sometimes air whispering from you gently, effortlessly,
like the cries from dreams lagging, dragging, and forgotten

it only seemed like a tease, the clashing of our complements,
the masking of our compliments
because of the experiences of our separate advantages

if life is not the first breath, but the breathing,
then neither is it about what you have left to give
but what you are leaving
So how much would you lose or have
you lost in waiting during this, our time?
Have the failures been many, the disappointments great?

because when the sun and clouds roll down to the ground,
to the edge of the world and to the ends of our lives,
we can be just as strong in our, with our weaknesses
as we are with our strengths...

     ...that are just incidental and accidental to the way we live..."

*"...it is the journey and not the destination that extends our pity
to the point that we are infatuated with it just for a moment..."*

Friends and Strangers (STOURY, (OUR STORY), Part VI)

we were acquainted long ago
sometime between youth and details
when we listened to a language of blind theories and ideals
and our practice was quite arbitrary

we were scared once--
we let the fear take hold for a moment
and yet this energy carried us forward
towards our oneness

we shared personal ways and means
and remembered nothing old or obsolete about each other
we noticed first the insides and then out,
our hearts darkened but not dulled by
the unconcerned shadows of this world

in this small, crowded place
'separate' does not exclude and
'together' does not isolate our union
but if we recognize and establish
our the center and the universe, we will respect the focus,
instead of the discovery and we may find our imperfections
perfectly acceptable and as challenging
as we'd prayed they would be

...and we think that this is how we are supposed to be..."

VII. RECONCILIATION

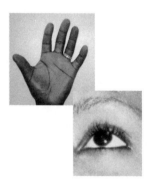

"...we have become what we have feared, comfortable and resistant
to further sharing, compromise, or happiness...

Are We Beautiful? (A Little Deception Among Friends, Part VII)

we answer the way we answer not as a matter of yes and no but of
how and where, when our objectivity is suspect and we salvage
simple, personal sentiments until we realize
that we have turned ourselves the wrong way

we hear those voices so little yet so strong because the background is
so vast and storied, but through these disciplined dreams and
dreaming, we replenish our reserves with research and new learning

within our hybrid nation, we are dimensional but no less accountable
and we need not be affirmed with others' endorsements. we are like
mountains merging with the skies and clouds and as the passages of
months, evaporating as dew into the southern May morning

how close is the emotional to the ethereal to the spiritual? casually or
causally, we are scared of, through, and about ignorance, always right
behind whomever is going to be first; and so much for the peace, for
we must first keep the strength so that we might fight for it,
if and when this becomes necessary

but despite the dilemma of our loss and how we are introspective only
when we need to search for reasons, our organization distracts and
detracts from a true leisure, a new, exclusive order and luxury
we want now to internalize and exhibit what we have lived through,
because the further we are away from what we forbid, the more
intriguing it seems and this pressure is overwhelming and irresistible

our minds must come together to celebrate our inability to fix the
problems *around* us, doing our best to understand the problems *about*
us without compounding or compressing the impressions we have
made thus far---we should expect the results to keep getting worse
and worse until we reconcile what we have done with what we can do

...the point of decision and separation of what we know from what we feel,
of what we want from what we need, and of what we deserve from what we accept..."

"...This is not a place for children,
but here we are looking wildly into each other's eyes...

Eve's Garden (This Is Heaven)

This is heaven, the first part
and we will celebrate the birth of you essentially here
wholly now that we see all that you are to become
flourishes and finishes found in this place,
however pleasant and present
just passed into the past through an
evolving door that took us forward through
our shame and misery, fear and worry
and our contentedness

was it nice where we used to live,
where the air was congested and confused and great lies
and deception spiraled up about us in our search?
But now we sow together and we have more than enough wheat and
"what" to warm ourselves with
you are the expression of thought, courageous
straining vines of life reaching beyond the proper confinement that
you understand, believe, and know about us

we were not prepared to enjoy what is now at our disposal
and we must be careful not to dispose of these blessings
while our ignorance clouds our vision
it may rain sometimes through these trees
but at least we know that it is just water
just like our tears
and it doesn't pelt
but it melts
into our grounded and tilled souls
the soil of our Heaven

...faltering and failing so young,
following each other out of the corners of our lives-- united, but unsure..."

"...But I keep looking behind and around myself, yet never ahead...

If and When (...since now)

At the end of the bottom line lie
our untested testimonials, like a sad mass
resounding and sounding like a chorus, a cadence behind the rhythm
like us, the different pages, the new and old stages,
are like cages now, though we can visit and feed each other
just enough to burnish an appetite

what are the chances of our next coincidence,
now that the odds are even?
I now sit where you stood, but does that make it fair?
can we still care and swear to an affair
that never quite suits either one of us..?

How far will our conspiracy go and how indelible will we be,
once we contribute to our
recitation of the trance, the dance where we
follow no particular ordination,
just a randomly sudden, terribly becoming
way of telling each other about our latest broken news

we have collected our impressions and hesitations
into stray thoughts, the ornate twinkle and glitter of callow
tributes that repair us hard to sleep
where we can see snow falling any time we want
without it being so close and cold
without the quick switches and introductions
without the loyalty and guilt
or the negligible noises and changes
that prevent us from distinguishing *here* from *now*,
this from that, since from sense
and If and When

...that which comes is never certain,
though I am certain of those things that are past and painful..."

"...this is the way we truly begin...

INTIMACITY, Part II

Somewhere near the precipice
I had once challenged and then resigned
I heard love

So instead of disrupting the mountains
distant ahead of me
I meekly bemoaned an absence extended

I retired from the imbalance of our fears and spirits
to a sensitivity greater than the love
we only speak of
and seldom realize

This is how it does begin
when we understand without listening
and speak without saying
more than the eyes and flesh allow

I now hold your thoughts as my wishes
and you caress my life with wisps of your breath
I find the hills level with the truth,
with heaven, with you
and I love you clearly
for the difference you make
in me, in you, in time, in pity
in this intensity, timid and torrid
this intimacy

...and begin to receive whatever it is we think we want and what we truly need..."

"...the beat and clock of calm winds, warm air...

Evocation: creating pleasure

perhaps it is selfish
to derive pleasure from another's satisfaction
somehow it is both good and bad
and the priorities shift from one to the other

to make water, for instance
you press your hands together
and pray like rain

and to make friends
you pressure some aspects of
yourself in return for the impression on others,
an expression you can use
until it is devoured or discovered or denied

but to make love
you relinquish obsession
and concentrate on the fulfillment,
not the action
until the differences release and collapse into one shared duration

and all this creation develops nothing material,
this is unseen yet real
especially upon the fear, the sensation,
and the congregation
of true pleasure

...and other subtle motions and mentions..."

"...and I didn't have time for patience; I didn't see or hear all at once...

Last Night (At Home, Part One)

the quiet times have been few
and far between
we have them now, though separately

We are bound with only the sounds of home,
the sounds of our music
the echo of our song
through a weakening volume of sadness
we become stronger
through the chorus that
reminds us
that we have returned
and were never really away

I believe in you and live in your spirit and light
--it seems I've been up all night
having you show me patience is not purgatory
but an envelope yet untitled and unopened

And the we indulge the temptation of reaching
almost all the way out
to that part of us that will complete us
and that may also hurt
but we develop into an acceptance of each other's movements and
moments--the very freedoms that brought us together--
And now we find ourselves
at home
with each other
at last

...and I missed the promise that you made to me the first time..."

"...to the darkness, the light and to the light, the truth...

PₑACE (STOURY, (OUR STORY), Part VII)

at the end of the beginning, we have run into a mix instead of
amok and spoken words that nestle and wrestle on our brows
like leaden leaves leaving their trees and fighting, lighting to cover
newly plowed ground And so luckily we have begun to stop gorging
ourselves on all of the fruit we can reach right now--we are
choosing to eat less and reach beyond "higher"

there is a glow under the distance where it has not rained as it has
here--we can't prove fire in the pouring rain without a little shelter
to burn down--that place we thought of, those streets of another
life and paradise were paved with pot-holed old gold and a
smoother, cruder strife and just the usual miracles of consequence
We were ready to get set and go with the best of those things that
do not, could not sustain us and now we are found similar or sound
familiar to and through each other for we, formerly, suffered for
trinkets and crumbs but now we succumb only to truth, trust and
deeper drums

We can hear more than we can see and we can see much more
when we eliminate the sound, whether noise or narration--we can
distinguish between time lines and timeliness, between clipped
aspiration and anticipation, short puffs and quick pouts
and the devoted, awakening breaths of patience there should be
peace in this space and space in this peace, personal infinities that
do not shape our faces into stupid smiles of sympathy,
susceptibility, shame or discomfort, a rather lonely chaos of voice
and script of two in the morning--like at two in the morning...as we
wiggle and squirm comfortably, subconsciously, and obviously in
love--Not in a house or a home--but in how we become and define
and refine who we are to be...so we draw from the cup of this
friendship, gently, quietly, cautiously, because we do not know how
many more times this will come, how much we will need or if we
can get more
of this peace, at this pace

...to the truth, the righteous and to this, the Glory..."

VIII. PERFECT UNION

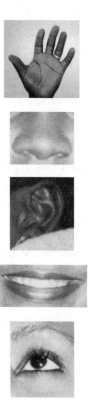

"...did we see ourselves coming or did we watch where we went...

Fields of Visions (A Little Deception Among Friends, Part VIII)

where we stand, accused and corrected
is where we built and then rose above
the emotive seconds and sections of a love that
should support our freedom and separation

is it, was it, murder or some sticky slick sort of preventative
medicine, like sand in a glass jar of vaseline floating in a spill of oil,
spoiling towards the beach, an invasion of our disdain,
discomfort and indifference
Honest in our deceit about today and yesterday,
our anger has crested into repulsion and pity
and we just cannot say no to the pleasure of the pain anymore

we are a thousand hidden under and beneath one tree
we are the forest, then, and still we don't see
even when one leaf falls
even when the least of us calls
we just absorb one another
Who will grieve for us and about our own--
the silly rich and cruel will have more water than we do,
but their sun is too hot for them, too
and we'll be right here under the boughs of our bowels and bowed
heads, too far below to be worried about...

We can condemn the explanations, even after we've offered no new
answers ourselves, terminally uncomfortable with this expression,
but not like strangers--more like tourists in our own, old town,
unfamiliar as it is until it is remembered:
the quiet places to dance, think, and talk, and the how and why
we were truly born here--

But our reflections are slow drips of stain and color
and we revel in the appearance of trails, but not in the direction of
the effort-- we are (at) each other's secrets--
our subtle hints and innocent comments contribute to a pain
that we have grown to expect and welcome
Moreover, we know less about this than when our wishes became
fears, when we stood nearer our one, true communion

the lonely should be out where they could at least meet each other
Or is the "in" of insecurity where they tell their stories in strange
order, so that no one can understand the sequence or
the sense of their complex requests?
It is here in their own shade, in their choices of people and
excesses,
that has them inhibited, their movement stagnated
by this bitterness but without proper knowledge or access

Do we really need another silent speaker for those who are weaker,
a "blinder-finder" to grope at those of us
who already *know* we are lost?
We have been misunderstood by the misled--
they knew we had these problems and many others
and we were all strangers before we met each other's glances,
gazes, and distorted views
can what has been more divided be now more united?
Maybe we have flattened our world
and our individual wills just enough so that
we can see more of each other
without straining too hard
through the several levels
of our distrust
and disbelief

...to understand where we would go next...?"

"...revelations are born of revolution and during periods of sacrifice and deprivation...

Mornings As If Always

we are as distinguishable as rain, mist, and fog,
our brows and lips moisten as we browse and lapse into a
contented
combination of arrangements and anxieties
the first wish is for the reunion of support and choice
an intimate, intricate inertia resulting from the ways we agree
but do not connect
and our lack of facts imparts a protective conspiracy
of silences, whistles and whispers,
often offending but intending to please

So though we are elated--we do love you and me and us
we are skittish and skirt certain issues
we knew we were falling from the time we started to unravel,
negotiating through our deferments and respect
the poor, tattered remnants of our traditional and symbolic
pedestals reveal the alliance, dalliance and decay into a primitive
discourse of simple, amorous and moronic motion

we continue into friendship after I have discovered what I like
about you and you, what you admire about me--
we grow into relationship after I discover what I like about you and
you, what you admire about me
despite what we know we hate about each other

we are impeded but never stopped in any way, though our house
and the family lacks the fullest possible structure, warmth and
composure that it could have, that it should have, as it should be...

...on the bridge between success and succumb..."

"...We have to choose back, also, regardless of the differences of home and potential..."

Push (No Questions)

we fire early and often announcing our intentions by relieving the
nervous habits that relax us and we keep thinking about movement
to redemption, to re-station ourselves deeply enough, straight
enough, strong enough to withstand the violations, the bent
overtures that resemble some semblance of necessity

our growing sin convinces us to stand alone and by the instruments
that will take us home to die--these are not the notes that naturally
place us at ease, but these are easier for us to listen to

we remember to forget the things that we were supposed to know,
appearing suddenly alert and we are never without an answer
we follow routes that run straight like the late creeping and
crowding of legions into something like the sea-- this is not our
world; we are branched, not tunneled, not brooked or dammed,
but our conclusions have been damned before our reasoning can
ever grow-- we are spinning into corners, and not just states, of
being; whether praying in groups or speaking in tongues,
our exceptions create rules and adjustments from the seamy, seedy
pretentiousness all around us and the result is a tingling, painfully
raw exposure to the loud, calloused and calling names and voices
that are our own

are they ribbons or shields, announcements or excuses, these
positions we promote and proclaim? we touch and scratch with
digits dirty from a lack of diligence--neither detergents nor
deterrents keep us clean of the habits we must defeat within...but
how can we let go before we have gained control? The tight, crisp
restrictions are provoked, then revoked and we are yoked by the
jealousy caused by our illusions

we point and fix, temper and tamper ever more with a
procrastination that justifies our hesitation and suspicion--we are
only babies in peril, lying supine and prone to the punching and
spitting and pitting and pushing of our spirits against obstacles
that exist Only for us to knock them down

...but there is no fear as great as that which keeps us where we have been..."

"...we shall push or pull, focus or divert as we must...

Home (At Home, Part Two)

my grandfather's dreams were light on his brow
the sun's shine on this man,
this wall that had withstood the time
of injustice and confinement
But the keys,
the individual answers to the questions and
inquisitions,
he held them and recounted their statements,
their stories of past and present
somehow the symbols revealed
more than I could witness
But as I saw devotion and faith travel from this
man's eyes to his fingertips,
I remembered that the finest ideas
and approaches to life were gifts and considerations
taken for granted and constantly pursued,
provided by the Image and Reflections around me,
surrounding and educating my soul

...on what we believe we are and were always meant to be..."

"...pain and trepidation still live...

This Is Grace (STOURY (OUR STORY), Part VIII)

And you welcome me homeward
after and from beneath all the carelessness I, we, could muster
We stand close and far enough away to
be bold about each other's daily occurrences

it is an effortless, silken sluice back into you
now that time and habit have made the argument conspicuous
like careful whispers between good and bad friends
we are limber and enabled enough to make these dynamic leaps
--you are still, evidently, fortunately stronger than I am
because you recover and recover me so elegantly,
encouraging me to let the words paint while we watch and wait

in isolation and exile we have strung together these apartments
full of depth and not of ourselves, but with the pieces of us, split
vertically, horizontally, and irregularly across, growing alike, not like
with resignation, capitulation and unlike anything we could ever
explain, but with destiny and an entwined destination

Our bodies fly together when we are there, but way behind the
closeness we have shared, so close that we are passing through each
other at times, so completely amoebic and without lines or bounds,
periods or dashes between that would separate the tickle in my ear
from the hint of your eye; our acceptance is the accentuation of these
sentences and words that taper and explode, receiving and
transmitting engagements within and around the curves of
recognition
and this grace is how we melt around the corners of each other

Because of certainty and circumstance (both)
we protect ourselves and others from the romance of each other
we cannot describe what we do--the trivial, simple
connotations that spell out the senses and tenses finish us without a
flawlessness that we are yet, still, very happy to be without

it is this grace, the little bit of gravity that pulls us otherwise,
unaware, inattentively together, the elixir that soothes and smooths
this arrangement of guilt, animosity, anguish, and disgust and
compels us, by the courage of the caress and nothing more, nothing
less than these nuances that connect, not the nuisances that distract--
we have been at the point of removal and renewal,
vibration and dictation before

Grace, deep and fragile like sadness
the enlightened and un-lightened versions that are close
to the personal and privately warm moistness we do not like to talk
about, because our minds are open only to what we enjoy now,
this coasting rise and flow of energy,
of our awareness and anticipation

this grace, and you comprise the essence of the best parts of life itself
almost as if through ether or by osmosis
we make ready, draw, and smash together pretty music and sincere
minds to please, wait, or break the blurred edges of this abject silence

the taste and taint of sequins and sequences during these days of
grace draped in greatness, uncomfortably heavy, weighty, and hefty
because we are all God's children with the devil within, just trying to
keep it together until we can get certain help, like before now when
we used to get into a lot less trouble when we knew a lot less and we
did not know the danger because we *just did not know*

but now we accept the parts of us that are so shallow
that when we wallow there long enough we still get very, very wet
And given more time and enough rope,
we will extend our grace, perhaps tempt our fate just a little,
finally choosing to give up some of our freedom for the security we
need, for when they and we inevitably collide and do not coincide,
for we, individually, are not as warm as *we* are,
for we will not ever be as cold as we once were,
for the grace we now share
Graces us here, now, and there

> *...and they eventually pass as thoroughly,*
> *as thoughtfully as we keep, stay, and retain..."*

"...it is the me that I long to see and understand in you, but it is more of the connection than conceit,...

Remembering To Need To Believe and Deceive
(A Little Deception Among Friends in the STOURY (OUR STORY))
(The Culmination)

...we exhaustingly seek to acquire the beauty
of others that we do not yet know how to
represent or respect *in ourselves*
We just want to be closer to the air,
to get more of the substance that
we think has eluded us
yet it is all around us, ever present and forgotten

we have lost too many arguments with ourselves
as we try to reason with the disappointment
of our pace
which develops in us our patience and peace

we are careful not to sit down too hard
or jump up too quickly to run immediately after that
which we have neglected to plan for, look for or follow;
but if all of our friends do rush over that cliff, we will be saved
by the bed of their bodies found at the bottom of our trust

Sometimes when we part the way we do,
parts of us never return
so we need and take more flesh than blood, thinking this will last,
to take us, sustain us, to the back of the end of the illusion,
the side we may not have taken the time to think on--
and if we did not think, is there still thought?
And what is forever was yesterday and we missed it and
the opportunity to save more than ourselves..?

...the collection of us without the confusion of all the others..."

"...we are still children and new, young students...

NEXT FOREWORD

Thank you! to all of you who have contributed, directly and indirectly, to this vision and blessing. I am only deceived by the measure of how I have hurt or helped you, my friends. I am not deceived, however, by the stories you have enriched me with. I hope they improve, become, and remain ours...Stay Tuned!

Derek

...in our actions and our deeds and in our needs..."

"...About the Author...

Derek Van Johnson is a successful soldier, businessman, entrepreneur, and writer. He attended elementary school in Amityville, New York where he was born. He completed junior high and high school in Dayton, Ohio before returning to New York to attend college. He received and accepted his appointment to the United States Military Academy at West Point, New York, graduating in 1984 with a Bachelor of Science in General Engineering and a concentration in Foreign Languages. He subsequently served for nearly 10 years in the United States Army as an Infantry Officer. He was an Airborne Ranger, Jumpmaster, Pathfinder, and Expert and Combat Infantryman serving two tours of combat (Panama, 1989/90 and Saudi Arabia, 1990/91). He began his business career as an Operations Research and Systems Analyst and progressed into various positions such as Information Technology Systems Analyst, Business Systems Engineer, Marketing/Client Solutions Manager, and Marketing Director with various Fortune 500 and Inc. 500 companies. He has also created his own company to serve as the foundation for his family's prosperity and financial independence and to fulfill his potential and responsibility to God.

...There is Only One God..."

ORDER FORM

Please send ___ copies of A Little Deception Among Friends (The Short sTOURy (OUR story) Conversations) at $14.95 per copy (check or money order only):

$14.95 x ____ copies = _____ (sub-total)

(Sub-total)_____ + (Sub-total x applicable sales tax) =
$_____ (total amount enclosed)
Please send the copies to:

NAME_____

ADDRESS_____

CITY/STATE/ZIP_____

PHONE (optional)_____
EMAIL_____

□ Please check here if you would like more information on this book, the author, or regarding One Fear One God One Life™ productions.
----
please detach or duplicate the order form above and mail to:

1FEAR GOD LIFE ™

One Fear One God One Life™ Publishing
(a division of S.A.I.N.T. International, Inc.)
107 South West Street, Suite 285
Alexandria, Virginia 22314-2824
phone: 703.929.2164/2165
email: VanSaint @ aol.com; Lisa Saint @ aol.com

ORDER FORM

Please send ___ copies of A Little Deception Among Friends (The Short STOURY (OUR story) Conversations) at $14.95 per copy (check or money order only):

$14.95 x ____ copies = _____ (sub-total)

(Sub-total)_____ + (Sub-total x applicable sales tax) = $_____
(total amount enclosed)
Please send the copies to:

NAME_____

ADDRESS_____

CITY/STATE/ZIP_____

PHONE (optional)_____
EMAIL_____

☐ Please check here if you would like more information on this book, the author, or regarding One Fear One God One Life™ productions.

----

please detach or duplicate the order form above and mail to:

1 FEAR GOD LIFE ™

One Fear One God One Life™ Publishing
(a division of S.A.I.N.T. International, Inc.)
107 South West Street, Suite 285
Alexandria, Virginia 22314-2824
phone: 703.929.2164/2165
email: Van Saint @ aol.com; Lisa Saint @ aol.com